EXCEPT THE LORD BUILD THE HOUSE

A Blueprint for Living a Christian Life

by

Dr. Trevor Williamson

Author Profile

Bishop Dr. Trevor Williamson, the founder and senior pastor of Trinity Global Cathedral in Nassau, Bahamas, is also a well-known motivational and inspirational speaker. His words of wisdom, edification and encouragement have inspired countless individuals to inculcate a positive attitude in life and reaffirm their faith in the Lord. Bishop Williamson ministers to the total man. He firmly believes in these lines: "For the Spirit of God is upon me, I will fear no evil, for the Word of the Lord comforts me." His book *Except the Lord Build the House* is an engaging meditation on the power of faith in modern life.

Table of Contents

Acknowledgement

First and foremost, I would like to thank my wife, Pastor Sharon, for standing beside me throughout these past twenty-seven years. She has been my inspiration, my motivation and my number one supporter. My wife continues to help me to excel by encouraging me to improve my knowledge and move toward the things God has planned for me. She is my pillar of strength, and I dedicate this book to her.

To my children, my dad Elder King Williamson, my mom the late Daisy Williamson, other family members, including my in-laws—thank you for your continued support, I really do appreciate you and your support.

Special thanks to Elder Andrea Pratt and Ms. Arthellia Powell Isaacs who encouraged me as I wrote this book.

To my Papa and Mentor, the late Dr. Myles Munroe, who was a great inspiration to me. Each time

I entered his presence, he would always greet me with the question, "Are you reading?" He always wanted me to excel and move ahead.

To Pastor Dave Burrows, the present Senior Pastor of Bahamas Faith Ministries, for your continued encouragement.

Special thanks to the Trinity Global Cathedral family in Nassau Bahamas—the greatest members ever, who have supported me and my family over these past twenty-one years.

Most of all, I want to thank God, my Heavenly Father, because without Him I wouldn't be able to do any of this.

Introduction

A few years ago, I embarked upon the journey of fulfilling God's assignment of building a sanctuary. Of course, I made it a point to obtain the best contractors and carpenters, along with other skilled workers. I knew that the quality of the work depended on the experience and detailed work of the builder. I carefully sought out workers who had proven track records and who would not take the money without completing the job, who were trustworthy. Many of you must have done the same when building your dream homes. You must've also realized that the soundness of the whole house depends on its foundation. If the contractor does not ensure the foundation is excellently built, it can jeopardize the entire structure. Sooner or later, cracks will appear. I live in a country prone to hurricanes, therefore, if the foundation is not strong, the building may even start to sink. The quality of the building is highly dependent on the competence and integrity of the contractor.

God is the Master Builder with a proven track record. It was God who gave Noah the specifications for building the ark that withstood enormous adversities and weathered the storm. It was also God who designed the world, with wonders such as Mount Everest, the Grand Canyon, Victoria Falls and the Glass Window Bridge in the beautiful archipelago of the Bahamas. Last, but certainly not the least, it was God who created the human body in all its splendor.

This very same God wants us to seek His guidance in building our lives, families and nations. In doing this, we will be able to withstand all adversities and rest knowing that after this short life is over, we can enjoy eternity with Him.

This book emphasizes the importance of building on a solid foundation, that of Jesus Christ. It is a book for the young as it teaches the importance and fruitfulness of living a life built on the teachings of Christ. It is also a book for the young at heart as it underscores the importance of legacy and of training the next generation to be Kingdom Ambassadors.

Block 1
Life: A Life of Labor Without God is in Vain

The last words people say before dying are often viewed as very significant. On his death bed, Cardinal Borgia (1492–1503) stated, *"I have provided in the course of my life for everything except death, and now alas, I am to die unprepared."* It is also said that the famous reggae singer Bob Marley's last words were *"Money can't buy life."*

Like King Solomon, the man who was blessed with profound godly wisdom, these men recognized that the many things we place the greatest value on are nothing but vanity. In the book of Ecclesiastes, King Solomon spoke on numerous occasions of the foolishness of pursuing happiness through worldly pleasures, riches, power, fame, lust and passion and finally came to the conclusion that the purpose of men is to *"...fear God, and keep his commandment for this is the whole duty of man"* (Eccl. 12:13).

In Psalm 127:1, Solomon again speaks on the fruitlessness of a life lived without God. He begins by stating, *"Except the Lord build the house, they labour in vain that build it…"* According to The Messenger Bible, Psalms 127:1 reads *"if God doesn't build the house, the builders only build shacks."* If God is not in control of your life, what you are doing in your life is likened to building a shack. Shacks are easily destroyed by storms or adverse conditions. They are not strong or sturdy, although they sometimes appear to be so.

In life, we will all face adversities and have our dark moments; however, a life built on a solid foundation, the Word of God, stands during adversity and also bears the promise of an eternal reward.

In Mathew 7:24–27, Jesus says, *"Therefore whosoever heareth these sayings of mine, and doeth them, I will liken him unto a wise man, which built his house upon a rock: And the rain descended, and the floods came, and the winds blew, and beat upon that house; and it fell not; for it was founded upon a rock."*

My 83-year-old father suffered the loss of his wife and five children; however, he still has joy and peace. What is his secret? With the guidance of God, his life is built on a firm foundation—the principles of Jesus Christ!

One of my wife's favorite hymns is "On Christ The Solid Rock I Stand All Other Ground is Sinking Sand," written by Edward Mote, a Baptist Minister, in 1834.

During the death of loved ones and other major crises we may face in our lives, we can rest assured that Christ, the rock of all ages, is unshakable. Even when friends walk out of our lives, He will never leave us or forsake us. We can boldly declare, "My hope is built on nothing less than Jesus' blood and righteousness!"

Jesus went on to describe those who choose to rebel and refuse to build their lives on the Word of God. He states in Matthew 7:26–27, "***And everyone that heareth these sayings of mine, and doeth them not, shall be likened unto a foolish man, which built his house upon the sand; And the rain descended, and the floods came, and the winds blew, and beat upon that house, and it fell; and great was the fall of it.***"

Are you like the wise man who built his house on the rock or like the foolish man who built his house on sand? Do you respond to adversity with a sense of despair or hopelessness? A foundation built on God can give peace that surpasses human understanding (Philippians 4:7).

A life built on the Word of God is a Spirit-led one, and God will place a song or scripture in your heart during your darkest hour. As He says in Isaiah 43:2, ***"When you pass through the waters, I will be with you; and when you pass through the rivers, they will not sweep over you. When you walk through the fire, you will not be burned; the flames will not set you ablaze."***

Just as the Lord was the fourth man in the fiery furnace in which Shadrach, Meshach and Abednego were bound, Jesus is with you in your situation.

As mentioned previously, Psalm 127 states ***"Except the Lord build the house, they labour in vain that build it…"*** In the scriptures, the word "labor" often means hard work or toil. We know of so many famous persons who worked hard to amass great wealth but ultimately committed suicide. We know of others who were in the prime of their lives, who had successful careers and everything going for them, but whose lives were cut short by death.

And then there are countless others who have worked hard all their lives to acquire wealth only to have it squandered away by their children after their death. Do not misunderstand me; money is not evil. Jesus said in His word, ***"Beloved, I wish above all things that thou mayest prosper and be in health even*** *as thy soul prospereth"* (3 John 1:2). However, God must have the first place in our lives. The scriptures firmly state, *"For what shall it profit a man, if he shall gain the whole world, and lose his own soul? Or what shall a man give in exchange for his soul?"* (Mark 8:36, 37).

Many have great plans for their lives, but unfortunately God is not a part of their plans. A favorite scripture of my mentor, Dr. Myles Munroe, was *"Many are the plans of a man's heart, but it is the Lord's purpose which shall prevail"* (Proverbs 19:21).

In Luke 12:20 NKJV, Jesus tells the parable of a rich fool who, after a great harvest, decided that he would build a barn to place all his stuff in, then said to himself, *"Soul, you have many goods laid up for many years, take thine ease, eat drink, and be merry."* However, God said to this man *"Thou fool, this night thy soul shall be required of thee: then whose shall those things be, which thou has provided?"*

As a pastor, I have seen so many people struggle financially or in other areas of their lives, but as soon as God blessed them, they forsook him and are now idolizing the blessing instead of worshipping the Creator. The blessing now reigns supreme in their lives: *"Who changed the truth of God into a lie, and*

worshipped and served the creature more than the Creator, who is blessed forever" (Romans 1:25).

Many build their lives around the lust of the flesh, the lust of the eyes and the pride of life (1 John 2:16). In other words, priority is placed primarily on the physical realm and on instant gratification. Some people build their lives on their wealth, beauty, physical abilities, persuasive abilities and other talents. However, it does not matter what your gift is, if God is not in it, you are just wasting your time. This applies to both unbelievers and carnal Christians alike. According to the Messenger Bible, ***"It is useless to…work your worried fingers to the bone. Don't you know he enjoys giving rest to those he loves?"*** (Psalms 127:2).

Many people work themselves to an early grave. They get up very early to go on jobs, leave work late in the hopes of recognition and promotion, but neglect God, who has given them the job. And if they are unfortunate enough to lose their job, two or three persons are hired to replace them. People work all their lives to obtain things. Their primary focus is on things. They do not spend time reading God's Word, and it is so sad that although they are extremely early for work, if they do come to church at all, they come late. They do not realize that a single idea from God can take care of all their needs because *"It is he that giveth thee power to get wealth"* (Due. 8:18).

God does not want us to be lazy. However, He wants us to remember to seek Him first and make Him a priority not only when we get old but also in our youth, while we are strong: *"Remember now your Creator in the days of your youth, before the days of trouble come and the years approach when you will say, 'I find no pleasure in them'"* (Eccl. 12:1).

When you make God your priority, you will find that He will make your desires His priority. For believers in Christ who build their lives according to the principles of God and follow His direction, God has promised in 1 Corinthians 15:58, *"Your labour is not in vain."* Additionally, there are others, like myself, who also labor in the Word and in teaching (1 Tim. 5:17). Our labor shall also not be in vain.

We must ask the Holy Spirit to guide us in our decisions daily and ensure that we *"Seek first the kingdom of God and his righteousness"* (Matt. 3:33), and all other things will be given unto us. We will surely discover that as we obey the first and the greatest commandment, which is to *"...love the Lord your God with all your heart and with all your soul and with all your mind"* (Matt. 27: 37–38), all our needs will be supplied. The more we seek to know who God is, the more He will reveal to us who He has created us to be. God only wants what is best for us. He stated in Jeremiah 29:11, *"For I know the thoughts that I think toward you, saith the Lord, thoughts of peace, and not of evil, to give you an expected end."*

The Merriam Webster Dictionary defines building as *"The art or business of assembling materials into a structure."* Let us build our lives on the solid rock; doing so will ensure our labor is not in vain.

Block 2
Nation: The Master Key to Building a Strong Nation

King Solomon in Psalm 127:1 clearly states *"…except the Lord keep the city, the watchman waketh but in vain"*.

Many modern societies are plagued with societal ills such as murder, corruption, gang violence, theft, witchcraft, abortion, divorce, teen pregnancy, suicide and so on. The founding fathers of many of our countries attempted to build our nations and their laws on godly principles; however, the more "sophisticated" we became, the more we scoffed at these principles and rid ourselves of many of the values, such as daily prayer in schools, which had made us the great nation we are now. This has led to a decline in morality in our society and its destruction at the very foundation.

What does the Word of God say about building a strong nation or strengthening a weak one? In 2 Chronicles 7:13–14, the Scriptures declare, *"If my*

people, which are called by my name, shall humble themselves, and pray, and seek my face, and turn from their wicked ways; then I will hear from heaven, and heal their land. " As Kingdom citizens, God holds us accountable for the healing of our nation. He states, ***"If my people…"*** We, who call ourselves Christians, are told to pray, fast and turn from wickedness, then promised that our prayers shall be heard and the problems in our land healed or fixed.

A nation is exalted when righteousness is important in the land. According to Prov. 14:34, ***"Righteousness exalteth a nation, but sin is a reproach to any people."*** It is so wonderful when righteous persons lead a nation. The scriptures put it this way in Proverbs 29:2, ***"When the righteous are in authority, the people rejoice; but when the wicked beareth rule, the people mourn."*** We often hear people say, "Politics is a dirty business." Can we have righteous politicians? I believe we can—persons who build their lives on the Solid Rock, Jesus Christ, and who possess integrity, compassion and humility.

Is your nation in a state which seems beyond repair? With God, nothing is impossible. On many occasions, the nation of Israel fell into moral decay, but God delivered them. They were in an abject state when God set the prophet Ezekiel in a valley of dry bones and asked him whether the bones could live again, then told Ezekiel to prophesy to the dry bones. God breathed on the bones, and they were covered with skin, and they lived. The same can happen to your country. Spiritual awakening can occur in our nations. Revivals can take place. Righteousness can be exalted in our nations. All is not lost. We simply need to return to the old landmark. I'm not talking about going back to the manual way of doing things. No, I am talking about not forsaking the godly principles we built our nations upon.

We often hear the Bible talk about watchmen watching over the city. It was the duty of those watchmen to stay awake and alert on the walls of the city and look out for any enemy who might try to invade the city during the night or day. According to Ezekiel 33:6, ***"But if the watchman see the sword come, and blow not the trumpet, and the people be not warned, if the sword come, and take any person from among them, he is taken away in his iniquity, but his blood will I require at the watchman's hands."*** As Kingdom citizens, we can watch over our city through prayer. However, it is well known that prayer meeting nights are the smallest services in most churches. People no longer want to come out to pray.

God's word says that ***"Except the Lord keep the city, the watchman, waketh but in vain."*** If the nation is not built on Christian principles, all armies, police forces, defense forces and other armed forces will be working in vain. In fact, in many ways, nations are destroyed internally.

Let us, as sons and daughters of the King, recommit to praying for our nations and their leaders (both religious and political) and turn to righteousness and watch God bring about an unbelievable transformation in our nations.

Block 3
Children: Nurturing God's Rich Heritage

"Behold, children are a heritage from the LORD, the fruit of the womb a reward." Prov. 127:3 ESV

Children are a blessing and not a curse; assets, not liabilities. They are a heritage; in other words, a gift or reward from the Lord. Too many persons nowadays see children as a nuisance or a curse. They are one of the most wonderful gifts God has given to us. We must seek God's guidance in nurturing children to grow up to be effective Kingdom ambassadors and disciples of God.

God's love for children is without question. In fact, in Matthew 18:10, Jesus stated, *"See that you do not despise one of these little ones. For I tell you that in heaven their angels always see the face of my Father who is in heaven."* When the disciples tried to prevent persons from bringing their young children to Jesus, *"...he was very much displeased, and said unto them, 'Suffer the little children to come unto me, and forbid them not: for of such is the kingdom of God.'"* (Mark 10:14). Our love for children should similarly be without question. We do not know the great purpose God has in mind for each child. Of Mary's child, Satan was told by God, *"I will put enmity between you and the woman, and between your offspring and her offspring; he shall bruise your head, and you shall bruise his heel."* Each child is a gift from God with a cataclysmic potential waiting to be nurtured, then released.

Similar to the fruit that comes from fruit-bearing trees, children are regarded by God to be the fruit of the womb. They are His *"best gift"* (Prov 127:3 MSG). Even before the seed is implanted in the womb, God is concerned for the child, because as He told Jeremiah, *"Before I formed thee in the belly I knew thee; and before thou camest forth out of the womb I sanctified thee, and I ordained thee a prophet unto the nations"* (Jeremiah 1:5). Isn't it wonderful that before the seed is even implanted in the womb God knows the child! And He has a purpose for that child even before the mother gives birth!

The Master Builder creates each child with love according to the purpose He has in mind. As King David declared, *"I will praise thee; for I am fearfully*

and wonderfully made, marvelous are thy works; and that my soul knoweth right well" (Psalms 139:14).

Nowadays, there are many people who do not believe it is "fashionable" to have many children. There are many who feel children are just too expensive and if you want nice material things, its best to limit yourself to one or two! As early as in the Garden of Eden, God demonstrated His desire for mankind to reproduce when He blessed Adam and Eve and ***"said unto them, Be fruitful, and multiply and replenish the earth..."*** (Gen. 1:28). The Bible further states, ***"how blessed are parents who have their quivers full of arrows!"*** A quiver is an arrow holder. In this instance, the Bible is likening children to arrows and proclaiming that parents who have many children are greatly blessed. The blessing is not limited to the parents for ***"grandchildren are like the crown of the elderly..."*** (Prov. 17:6).

An arrow is usually considered to be a missile or a weapon. According to the Messenger Bible, ***"Like a warrior's fistful of arrows are the children of a vigorous youth. Oh, how blessed are you parents, with your quivers full of children! Your enemies don't stand a chance against you; You'll sweep them right off your doorstep."*** Your children can become your greatest defenders and supporters. They are reinforcement against the enemy! No, your enemies will not have a chance against you! Your children are your arrows. If someone were to hit my dad, Elder King Williamson, they may think they are dealing with one man; however, his arrows or children will leap to his defense. God will give you children who are courageous and will have the fortitude to walk right up to the devil and say to his face, "Try it!" People see you, but they do not know that behind your back is your quiver full of arrows!

In many instances, although you may not be able to complete the vision God has given to you, once they are well trained, your children will get the job done!

If you have toiled hard to raise your child according to godly principles, God will surely raise that child to become a financial blessing to you and a contributing citizen of the nation. Some of you may be reading this and saying, "But I do not have a child." However, although you do not have a biological son or daughter, you can have spiritual sons and daughters whose lives you have impacted to become assets to the Kingdom of God. My aunt, Elder Queenie Rose, was such a person. Although she did not have any biological children, she raised, nurtured and taught her spiritual sons and daughters to fear God and keep His commandments.

Children are a blessing regardless of the circumstances surrounding their birth. One of the greatest televangelists, James Robison, was the product of rape. However, today God has used him to be instrumental in feeding millions of people in Africa and around the world. If my dad or mum had decided to abort me, they would have aborted a blessing!

Some people come from dysfunctional homes and raise their children with the same dysfunction, which results in them becoming wayward. But God can still change things. Do not grow weary praying for your child, and continue to apply the blood of Jesus Christ over them, asking God to send persons in their path who will declare the Word of God and who they will listen to.

Take care of your children and watch over them. Put them in God's hand. See them as a ministry God has given to you. Whatever you can do for them, do it and watch them arise to be assets in society. Purpose in your heart to commit to praying for your family, and if you do not have an earthly child, remember the old saying "It takes a village to raise a child," and so raise up someone else's child in the fear of the Lord and for His great service.

Block 4
Rest: Rewards for Building According to God's Purpose

"It is vain for you to rise up early, to sit up late, to eat the bread of sorrows: for so he giveth his beloveth sleep." Proverbs 127:2

God created the world in seven days. Then, on the seventh day, *"….God ended his work which he had made and he rested…"* (Genesis 2:2). God does not work slaves! The Bible states that He gives His beloved sleep. We do not need to stay up all night worrying about situations such as overdue bills, family issues or problems on the job. We can rest in the knowledge that *"all things work together for good to them that love God, to them who are called according to his purpose"* (Romans 8:28).

My word to you is "Go to sleep!" Stop worrying about everything. God is still in control. Turn your problems over to God through prayer. Saint Augustine put it like this, *"Pray as though everything depended on God. Work as though everything depended on you."*

Yes, we are required to work, as faith without work is dead. However, it is also important for us to rest; there must be a balance in our lives. We must also learn to trust God, rest on Him and not get weary in *"well-doing for in due season we will reap if we faint not"* (Galatians 6:9).

God has a time of harvest for His saints. But there is also a time of rest. How do we enter into this rest which He has promised us? We do so through faith. According to Hebrews 4:2, *"For unto us was the gospel preached, as well as unto them: but the word preached did not profit them, not being mixed with faith in them that heard it."* This scripture refers to the Israelites who had seen God's great works after He delivered them out of Egyptian bondage but murmured and refused to trust Him and therefore did not enter Canaan—the promised land. Forty years later, the next generation, because of their faith in God, did enter that place of rest. Today, instead of obtaining salvation through work, we can *"rest in the finished works of Jesus Christ by faith"*.

Faith is our way of entering into God's rest. This does not mean we are to do nothing; we must yield ourselves to God. He is the Master Builder. For the Apostle Paul goes on to say, *"Let us, therefore, make every effort to enter that rest, so that no one will*

perish by following their example of disobedience" (Hebrews).

We must have faith in God even when we feel we cannot trace Him. According to the scriptures, ***"But without faith it is impossible to please him; for he that cometh to God must believe that he is, and that He is a rewarder of them that diligently seek him"*** (Hebrews 11:6).

Can a person confess Jesus Christ as their Lord if they do not believe He exists? It is impossible. This is one of the reasons why faith is crucial for believing in God. Furthermore, we must believe that He will reward us if we seek Him diligently. Seeking His face, not just His hands. If we build our lives according to God's purpose, He will surely reward us.

No matter what situations you face today, remember He gives His beloved sleep, for He is a God who neither slumbers nor sleeps. The two of you do not need to be up. Rest knowing your Heavenly Father has the situation under control.

Block 5

Legacy: Building a Rich Legacy for the Generations to Come

There are many rewards to building one's life on the principles of the Lord Jesus Christ, but the one I would like to focus on in this chapter is legacy.

There are many buildings worldwide which were built centuries ago but still exist today, such as the Great Pyramid of Giza (Egypt), the Parthenon (Greece) and the Colosseum (Italy). The handiwork of the builders has lasted many generations after their passing, and we still admire these structures today. Similarly, when you build your life on God's words, you can leave behind a godly legacy and positively impact future generations even after you are gone.

The Book of Proverbs declares *"A good man leaveth an inheritance to his children's children: and the wealth of the sinner is laid up for the just"* (Proverbs 13:22). In other words, the good that you do positively impacts your grandchildren and future generations and the wealth that is obtained unjustly ultimately ends up in the hands of the righteous.

There are many keys to leaving behind a rich legacy. One of the first is developing a vision. When Habakkuk was disturbed by certain things in his country, the Lord said to him, ***"Write the vision, and make it plain upon tables, that he may run that readeth it. For the vision is yet for an appointed time; but at the end it shall speak, and not lie. Though it tarry, wait for it; Because it will surely come, It will not tarry"*** (Habakkuk 2:2–3). The Messenger Bible states, ***"And then God answered: 'Write this. Write what you see. Write it out in big block letters so that it can be read on the run. This vision-message is a witness pointing to what's coming. It aches for the coming—it can hardly wait! And it doesn't lie. If it seems slow in coming, wait. It's on its way. It will come right on time'"*** (Habakkuk 2:2–3).

Having a vision and clearly outlining it is vital to leaving a rich legacy. The leadership expert John Maxwell stated that *"Good leaders must communicate vision clearly, creatively and continually. However, the vision doesn't come alive until the leader models it."* Before the Trinity Global Cathedral was built, I saw it. I clearly communicated my vision to others, and now they can see it before their own eyes. I also see future buildings, countless souls added to the Kingdom of God and a rich legacy.

If you do not have a clear vision or an understanding of God's purpose for your life, people will try to tell you who you are and what your purpose is. My question to you is "What do you see?" It is written in Proverbs 29:18 that ***"Where there is no vision, the people perish."*** Do you have a vision for your future generations? Do you see them impacting the Kingdom of God and having a positive influence on the nation? Have you communicated this to anyone? Do you have a plan for achieving this? Are you passionate enough to go after it? It is also important for us to see the bigger picture. You may ask what I mean by this statement. Your vision may be too small. Instead of a vision that is simply national, think global. Instead of just your children, think of the generations to come. Instead of the church, think of the Kingdom. For too long we have lived by the terms "you in your small corner and me in mine". It is time for us to broaden our vision and think about how we can leave a great legacy for our future generations spiritually, economically, culturally and in other areas. God often spoke to individuals about the impact He would have on their future generations because of the individual's obedience to His Word. He did this with both Abraham and David. He can also do this with you. God asked Jeremiah, *"'Jeremiah, what do you see?' And I said I see a branch of almond tree. Then the Lord said to Me, 'You have seen well for I am watching to perform My word'"* (Jeremiah 1:11–12). Ask God to give you a vision for your generation and He will surely watch over His Word and bring that vision to pass!

If we are to build a rich legacy, it is also critical for us to teach our children the commands of God and to testify to His marvelous works! Too often as parents we want to make life easier for our children. We do not want them to struggle as we did. Unfortunately, in many instances they do not know the value of certain things, the sacrifices they cost us and the greatness of the God who made everything possible for us. Joshua 4:21–23 declares, *"And He spake unto the children of Israel, saying, When your children shall ask their fathers in time to come, saying, What mean these stones? Then ye shall let your children know, saying, Israel came over this Jordan on dry land. Yes, God, Your God dried up the Jordan's waters for you until you had crossed."* We must continually tell our children about the God who has *"brought us from a mighty long way"*. The scriptures also speak of the importance of doing this in Psalms 78:4, which states, *"We will not hide them from their children, shewing to the generation to come the praises of the Lord,*

and his strength, and his wonderful works that he has built" and also admonishes us to do this in Deut. 6:7, declaring, ***"And thou shall teach them diligently unto thy children, and shall talk of them when thou sittest in thine house, and when thou walkest by the way, and when thou liest down, and when thou rises up."*** If we do not teach our children the things we are admonished to, over time a generation will arise that does not know God, as was the case in Judges 2:10: ***"After that generation died, another generation grew up who did not acknowledge the Lord or remember the mighty things he had done for Israel."***

Mentorship also plays a key role in leaving a rich legacy. Have you mentored anyone so that your vision can outlast you? There is nothing like Divine mentorship. There are persons who God has placed in your path to mentor. Jesus Christ was a perfect example of this principle. Over 2000 years ago, He discipled or mentored twelve men from diverse backgrounds and with distinct personalities. They spent time with Him, and He spoke to them in parables that others often did not understand. He taught them and then demonstrated the key principles of His Kingdom to them. He encouraged them but also rebuked them when necessary. He did not hold onto His position as mentor or leader over them longer than required— only three years. After the period of mentoring came to an end, He told them what their great commission was, then left them. Thousands of centuries later, we are still blessed because of His example of mentorship in all its perfection. He was the best example of an excellent mentor. Wonderful legacies can be left when you mentor an individual.

Be a good mentor to others through your actions and words and motivate others to reach their highest potential. People are watching you even when you do not know it. Over the ages, we have seen many evangelists and other persons who have been used by God to win millions of souls to Christ but who were mentored by someone, such as a parent, who may not be as well known. That parent has a rich legacy because of the role they played in mentoring that evangelist, resulting in so many souls being won for Christ. I am sure John Osteen, the founder of Lakewood Church, mentored his son Joel Osteen. Upon his death, his son became the pastor of the church, and in 1999, the church membership reportedly grew from 5,000 to 43,000 members! This is the power of good mentorship and an example of leaving behind a rich legacy. Jesus said these words to His disciples, ***"Verily, verily I say unto you, He that believeth on me, the works that I do shall he do also; and greater works than these shall he do, because I go unto my Father"*** (John 14:12).

Over the years, I have seen many great men and women of God go home to be with the Lord. However, I have also seen these great people pass the baton onto their spiritual sons and daughters, who, like Elisha, have a double portion of their leader's anointing. I am then reminded of the scripture ***"Verily, verily, I say unto you, Except a corn of wheat fall into the ground and die, it abideth alone: but if it die, it bringeth forth much fruit"*** (John 12:24).

Mentor your children, grandchildren and others and, after you are gone, their impact in the Kingdom of God and nationally may be greater than yours. Mothers, mentor your daughters. The Bible puts it this way, ***"That they may teach the young women to be sober, to love their husbands, to love their children, to be discreet, chaste, keepers at home, good, obedient to their own husbands, that the word of God be not blasphemed"*** (Titus 2:4–5). Also, men, mentor your sons: ***"Young men likewise exhort to be sober minded. In all things shewing thyself a pattern of good works: in doctrine shewing uncorruptness, gravity, sincerity, sound speech, that cannot be condemned; that he that is of the contrary part may be ashamed, having no evil thing to say of you"*** (Titus 2 6–8).

There are also persons God has placed in your life to mentor you. These persons are key to fulfilling

God's purpose for your life and impacting generations to come. The scriptures are full of examples of persons who understood the significance of their mentors, including Elisha (mentored by Elijah), Joshua (Moses) and perhaps even Ruth (Naomi). It was obvious to others that Elisha was the spiritual son of Elijah because Elijah's mantle was upon him. As Elijah and Elisha were about to leave Gilgal, Elijah told Elisha that he was going into Bethel and that he wanted him to remain in Gilgal, but Elisha's response to his mentor was *"Not on your life! I'm not letting you out of my sight!"* (2 Kings 2:2). So, they both went to Bethel. Later Elijah again asked Elisha to remain in Bethel and told him he would go on to Jericho. But once again Elisha was determined not to part with his mentor. His response was *"Not on your life! I'm not letting you out of my sight!"* (2 Kings 2:4 MSG). So, they both went to Jericho. Finally, Elijah said to Elisha, *"Stay here. God has sent me on an errand to the Jordan"* (2 King 2:6 MSG). Once again Elisha declared, *"Not on your life! I'm not letting you out of my sight!" And so the two of them went their way together."* (2 King 2:6 MSG). Shortly thereafter, the Lord took Elijah up in a chariot of fire, and Elisha receive his mantle which was a symbol of his ministry. Others knew that he had the spirit of a Son of Elijah when he was able to strike the mantle on the river and it parted in two just as it had parted when Elijah had struck it. Elisha spent time with his mentor and obtained the reward! Similarly, Ruth told her mentor, Naomi, that she would not leave her, but Ruth said, *"Don't force me to leave you; don't make me go home. Where you go, I go; and where you live, I'll live. Your people are my people, your God is my God; where you die, I'll die, and that's where I'll be buried, so help me God—not even death itself is going to come between us!"* (Ruth 1:16–17 MSG). All of these persons were blessed because they withstood the mentoring process. Mantles were passed on because these persons spent time with their mentor and endured the test.

Respect those who are mentoring you. Eli had certain shortcomings; however, Samuel still displayed respect towards him. Remember that your mentor has the knowledge you need to obtain. Spend time with your mentor, and remember the importance of listening. This may seem simple, but too often we miss an opportunity to receive vital information from our mentor because we continually interrupt them and fail to listen as they speak. Also, allow any criticisms to strengthen you.

I have been mentored by many Generals of the faith over the years, including Prophet T. B. Joshua of Lagos, Nigeria, Apostle Skip Horton of Douglasville, Georgia, as well as Bishop Neil C. Ellis, Apostle

Paul Butler, the late Dr. Myles Munroe, and Bishop Elkin Symonette, all four of whom are from Nassau, Bahamas. When I need information, I do not go to a novice. I go to someone who has been tried; a general, not a rookie. When I was a child, my dad, Elder King Williamson, awoke me daily at 3 a.m. in the morning to pray, but I did not disrespect him for doing this, and it is partly responsible for me growing into the man I am today. I am grateful for the mentorship I received from all of these mighty men of God. Serve your mentor and be faithful so that you are prepared for what God has in store for you. Carry on the legacy and the pattern of your mentor, but know that with God's help, you will be able to do greater works! Joshua spent years serving Moses and when Moses died, God told Joshua to ***"Give it everything you have, heart and soul. Make sure you carry out The Revelation that Moses commanded you, every bit of it. Don't get off track, either left or right, so as to make sure you get to where you're going"*** (Joshua 1:7 MSG). Joshua was able to build on the instructions of Moses and lead the children of Israel into the promised land.

When we look at persons who have left a legacy, what do they often have in common? Most of them have passion. Martin Luther King, Jr. is famously quoted as saying *"If you've got nothing worth dying for, you've got nothing worth living for."* Are you so passionate about your God-given assignment that you will not give up on the dream? No matter what you may be going through or who may be trying to deter you, continue to build your marriage, your nation, your church, your family, your business and declare as Nehemiah did—*"I am doing a great work, so that I cannot come down. Why should the work cease, whilst I leave it and come down to you?"* (Nehemiah 6:2–4).

There is a sport called hurdles in which the competitors are expected to leap over barriers and the one who finishes first without falling before the finish line and knocking over the barriers is the winner. Sometimes we face hurdles in life. But, like the athletes in this sport, we must continue to leap over each hurdle if we want to achieve our goal. Do not let the hurdles in life stop you. Continue to remain focused and passionate about the goal. Be reminded of the scripture, *"And let us not be weary in well doing: for in due season we shall reap, if we faint not"* (Gal. 6:9). Do not let anyone discourage you and, with God's help, you will leave a great legacy!

I would like to conclude by mentioning two scriptures of the Bible in addition to Psalms 127, which I believe are important if we are to understand the importance of building a rich legacy: Isaiah 58:12 and Isaiah 61. Isaiah 58:12 states:

> *"And they that shall be of thee shall build the old waste places: thou shalt raise up the foundations of many generations; and thou shalt be called, The repairer of the breach, The restorer of paths to dwell in."*

Similarly, Isaiah 61:4 states:

> *"And they shall build the old wastes, they shall raise up the former desolations, and they shall repair the waste cities, the desolations of many generations."*

God can raise you up to be known as the restorer of the breach. Yes, the foundations of your family or nation may have been destroyed, but God can raise you up to rebuild those foundations. Your family may have been dysfunctional for years, but God can raise you up to be a restorer of that familial breach. Some people have been used to destroy the lives of their children. Others are used by God to build up their children and future generations. Will you leave behind a legacy of generational curses or blessings? Will you be used by God to rebuild the destroyed foundations of your family life? Will you be known as the "repairer of the breach" by your family? You only have to look at Luke 1:37 to know that *"For with God nothing shall be impossible."*

As you build a rich legacy by following godly principles and teaching them to your children and grandchildren, your house will stand; just as a church is built on the Word of God, "...***the gates of hell shall not prevail against it***" (Matt. 16:18). Seek God's guidance through prayer in all that you do and make Him a priority in every area of your life including family life, finances and career and your life will not be lived in vain.

If you would like God's guidance in building your life according to His plans and purpose, join me in this simple prayer.

Heavenly Father, I come in the name of Jesus Christ, giving you all glory and honor as the Creator of all things. Father, I know that you created me with a plan and a purpose, and I come seeking your guidance in fulfilling that plan. Thank you, Father for protecting me thus far from the plans of the enemy. Thank you for sending your Son as a living sacrifice for my sins. Forgive me for every sin I have committed in thoughts, deeds and actions. Father, I recognize that except when the Lord build the house, they labor in vain that build it. I welcome your Holy Spirit into my life to give me the wisdom, knowledge and understanding that is needed to fulfill your purpose. Thank you for breaking every chain and destroying every yoke which has me bound. Anoint me to be used by you to restore broken areas in my family's life and in my nation. Father, I ask you to use me to mentor future ambassadors for your Kingdom, and I will be mindful to give you all the glory and honor. In Jesus' name. Amen.

About the Author

Bishop Dr. Trevor Williamson is a man after God's own heart, a man who stands for nothing but holiness and righteousness. He was born on Acklins Island, the Bahamas. Bishop Trevor began preaching at the age of seventeen during street meeting services with the Ebenezer Mission Baptist Church, Nassau, Bahamas.

Bishop Dr. Trevor Williamson is the Founder and Senior Pastor, along with his wife Sharon, of **"Trinity Global Cathedral"** located on Marshall Road opposite Faith Avenue, Nassau, the Bahamas.

He is a faithful and devoted servant to the work that God has called him to do. A gifted teacher and preacher, proclaiming the Word of God both nationally and internationally, he holds a Doctor's Degree in Theology.

Beside Bishop Dr. Trevor Williamson stands a great woman of God, **Pastor Sharon Williamson,** who works tirelessly by his side in the ministry.

Bishop Dr. Trevor Williamson is known as a Motivational and Inspirational Speaker. He speaks words of wisdom, inspiration and edification, and encouragement, which enhances and adds to the positive attitude of individuals, who he comes in contact with. Bishop Williamson ministers to the total man.

One of his favorite quotes is, "For the Spirit of God is upon me, I will fear no evil, for the word of the Lord comforts me."

www.ingramcontent.com/pod-product-compliance
Lightning Source LLC
Chambersburg PA
CBHW061314050726
47594CB00004B/1713